MIDWEST ECLOGUE

BOOKS BY DAVID BAKER

POETRY

Midwest Eclogue (2005)

Treatise on Touch: Selected Poems (2005)

Changeable Thunder (2001)

The Truth about Small Towns (1998)

After the Reunion (1994)

Sweet Home, Saturday Night (1991)

Haunts (1985)

Laws of the Land (1981)

CRITICISM

Heresy and the Ideal: On Contemporary Poetry (2000)

Meter in English: A Critical Engagement (1996)

MIDWEST ECLOGUE

poems

DAVID BAKER

W. W. Norton & Company   New York • London

For information about permission to reproduce selections from this book, write to
Permissions, W. W. Norton & Company, Inc., 500 Fifth Avenue, New York, NY 10110

Manufacturing by Quebecor Fairfield
Book design by Chris Welch
Production manager: Julia Druskin

Library of Congress Cataloging-in-Publication Data

Baker, David, 1954–
Midwest eclogue : poems / David Baker.—1st ed.
p. cm.
Includes bibliographical references.
ISBN 0-393-06090-X
1. Middle West—Poetry. I. Title.
PS3552.A4116M53 2005
811'.54—dc22
2005014596

W. W. Norton & Company, Inc., 500 Fifth Avenue, New York, N.Y. 10110
www.wwnorton.com

W. W. Norton & Company Ltd., Castle House, 75/76 Wells Street, London W1T 3QT

1 2 3 4 5 6 7 8 9 0

for Ann and Katie

CONTENTS

ACKNOWLEDGMENTS

These poems appeared in the following magazines, to whose editors I extend my grateful acknowledgment: *The American Scholar*, "Hedonism"; *Field,* "Post Meridian"; *Five Points*, "Alchemical Man," "Bedlam," "No One Said," "October Storm," "White Heron Pond"; *The Georgia Review*, "Hyper-," "Primer of Words"; *The Gettysburg Review,* "The Judas-Horse," "Slant Cut"; *The Michigan Quarterly Review*, "Midwest Eclogue"; *The Mid-American Review,* "White Violets and Coal Mine"; *The Nation*, "The Blue," "Monarchs Landing and Flying"; *The New England Review*, "Cardiognosis"; *The Paris Review*, "Melancholy Man"; *Ploughshares*, "The Evidence," "Winged"; *Poetry*, "The Spring Ephemerals," "The Waves"; *Slate,* "My Mother in Shock"; *The Southeast Review,* "Silo Oaks"; *The Virginia Quarterly Review,* "Late Pastoral"; *The Yale Review*, "Hunger."

I am grateful to the John Simon Guggenheim Memorial Foundation, the National Endowment for the Arts, and Denison University for their generous support and encouragement.

I sing of *Times trans-shifting.*
—*Robert Herrick*

If they have come for the butterflies then
bless their breaking hearts, but the young pair is
looking nowhere except each other's eyes.
He seems like he could carry them both
over the street on great wings of grief tucked
under his coat, while all around them float,
like wisps of ash or the delicate
prism sunlight flashing off the city glass,
the orange-yellow-black-wing-flecked monarchs.
Migrant, they're more than two dozen today,
more long-lived than the species who keep
to the localized gardens—they're barely
a gram apiece, landing, holding still for
the common milkweed that feeds their larvae,
or balanced on bridges of plume grass stalks
and bottlebrush, wings fanning, closing, calmed
by the long searchlight stems of hollyhock.
If they have come for the butterflies then
why is she weeping when he lifts her chin?
He looks like he's holding his breath back—
or is he trying to shed tears, too? Are
any left? He's got his other hand
raised, waving, and almost before it stops
the taxi's doors flare on both sides open.
Nothing's stirring in the garden, not us,
not the thinnest breeze among the flowers,
yet by the time we look again they've flown.

Then a stillness descended the blue hills.
I say stillness. They were three deer, then four.
They crept down the old bean field, these four deer,
for fifteen minutes—more—as we watched them

in the field, in the soughing snow. That's how
slowly they moved in stillness, slender deer.
The fourth limped behind the other three,
we could see, even in the darkness, as it

dragged its right hindquarter where it was
hit or shot. Katie sat back on her heels.
The dog held in his prints, or Kate held him,
hardly breathing at first. Then we relaxed.

Blue night descended our neighbor's blown hills.
And the calm that comes with seeing something
beautiful but far from perfect descended—
absolute attention, a fixity.

I say absolute. It was stillness.

In the books we gathered, the first theory
holds that the condition's emergence is
most common at age eight, if less in girls

than boys, or more vividly seen in boys
whose fidgets, whose deficit attentions,
like little psycho-economic realms,
are prone to twitches-turned-to-virulence,
anxieties palpable in vocalized
explosions—though now we know in girls
it's only on the surface less severe,
which explains her months of bubbling tension,
her long blue drifts and snowy distractions.
I say distractions. Of course I mean how,
clinically, tyrosine hydroxylase
activity—the "rate limiting enzyme
in dopamine synthesis"—disrupts, burns,
then rewires her brain's chemical pathways.

Let me put it another way. After
twenty-four math problems, the twenty-fifth
still baffles her, pencil gnawed, eraser-
scuff-shadows like black veins on her homework.

It's not just the theory of division
she no longer gets, it's her hot clothes, her
itchy ear, the ruby-throated hummingbird's
picture on the fridge, what's in the fridge, whose

socks these are, why, until I'm exhausted
and yell again. Until she's gone away
to her room, lights off, to sulk, read, cry, draw.
No longer trusting to memory, she

writes everything in her journal now, then
ties it with a broken strand of necklace.
Of her friends: *I am the funny one.* Mom:
She has red hair and freckles to. Under Dad:

I have his bad temper. I know. I looked.

In one sketch she finished, just before we
learned what was wrong—I mean, before we knew
what to call what was wrong, how to treat it,
how to treat *her*—she captured her favorite
cat with a skill that skips across my chest.
He's on a throw rug, asleep. The rug's fringe
ruffles just so. The measure of her love is
visible in each delicate stroke, from
his fetal repose, ears down, eyes sealed
softly, paws curled inward, to the tiger lines
of his coat deepened by thick textures
where she's slightly rubbed away the contours
with her thumb to winter coat gray. He's soft,

he's purring, he's utterly relaxed asleep.
One day, before we learned what was wrong,
she taped it to a pillow on my bed.
Terry Is Tired she'd printed at the top.

How many ways do we measure things by
what they're not. I say things. Mostly her mind
is going too fast, yet the doctors give her,
I'm not kidding, amphetamines—

speed, we used to say, when we needed it—
Ritalin, which wears off hard and often,
Adderal, which lasts all day though her food's
untouched and sleep comes late. The irony

is the medicine slows her down. She pays
attention, understands things. The theory
is, AD/HD patients "aren't hyper-
aroused, they're underaroused," so they lurch

and hurtle forward, hungry for focus.
Another theory says the brain's two lobes
are missized. Their circuits "lose their balance."
One makes much of handedness—left—red hair,

allergies, wan skin, an Irish past . . .

We watched four deer in stillness walking there.
Stillness walking, like the young blue deer hurt
but beautiful. In her theory of
division, Katie's started drawing them—
her rendering's reduced them down to three.
She has carefully lined the cut bean rows
in contours like the dog's brushed coat. Snowflakes
dot the winter paper. Two small deer stand
alert on either side of the hurt one
leaning now to bite the season's dried-up stems.
Their ears are perched like hands, noses up, tails
tufted in a hundred tiny pencil lines.
She's been hunkered over her drawing pad,
humming, for an hour. So I watch. I say
watch. I ask why she's made the little hurt
one so big. Silly. He's not hurt that bad,
she says. She doesn't look up. That one's you.

Half a life's wanting, the other's regret
is what she's painted in bold black letters
on a weathered plank. She's arranged fifteen
or twenty such marquees around their yard
—nailed to front-porch posts, propped along the trees—
aimed at angles to the road to give us
time to brood, breathe, and be thus instructed.
God Needs a Bird is a bright one, though two

feet further she has started Look o and run
out of room—this board is a brown wing
flashing through her squat apple tree, balanced
in the knotted limbs and squandered blooms.
For days cars have idled by, looking
for her, thin, blonde, thirty or so, who
won't talk now except in these messages.
How articulate her display, yet how

wrenching to see the woodshed board by board
melting off in the sunshine, honey-vines-
turned-ghost where she's ripping the west wall out.
They're coming! But who? Angels? Aliens?
Collectors? Old friends? Each is a savior
who might answer the one splintered marker
propped by the birdbath brimming with boots,
Husband Missing 5/22/02.

1.

This one wild enough to tame with enough
time, whose brown mane flicks to flame, and this one
roughed-up in the weather, winded, ruffled
and muscled, running like wind, hooves churning,
and two more, then three charging, galloping
over the blasted prairie hilltop grass—
burr-coated, mud-matted, nicked by hooves
in battle or mating's warrior moments.

2.

The thighs tighten—a canter in the ring.
The toe tips out to turn. Your hands above
the withers hold the reins, "as glass,"
lest the horse find meaning in a jostle . . .
The usual mode of taking the wild
horses is by throwing the *laso* whilst
pursuing them at full speed, and dropping
a noose over their necks—so Catlin writes—

3.

thus they are "choked down," until the horse falls
from want of breath, and lies helpless on the ground,
where it soon becomes docile and conquered.

Or "creasing." This is done by shooting them
through the gristle on the top of the neck,
which stuns them so they fall, and are secured
with the hobbles on their feet; after which
they rise again without fatal injury.

4.

I have loved you wild enough to hurt you.
I know this now. I have been docile, conquered,
dependent. The smallest movements matter.
Catlin paints the Mandan buffalo-men
—1832, upper Missouri—
flying, a few paces from the herd,
atop horses only lightly tamed by
a hand on the animal's nose, over

5.

its eyes, at length "to breathe in its nostrils."
Our love is furious and calm. Thus we
ride over the sweet-smelling earth neither
toward each other nor away. The horse, he writes,
yields gladly—. This one a flurry of dust.
This one nose down, tail flung, flying like foaming
water. And this one, the tame one, running
with the others, to lead them through the gate.

Mr. Clare has decided to walk home,
bluecaps under foot, maiden-loam, the green
abounding countryside in sudden song.
Four years with Dr. Allen and he's been
a vapour tossed into a nothingness
of noise, Fair Mead House and Leopard's Hill Lodge,
the Northampton General Lunatic

Asylum—such awful din to the rustic
poet shuffled among them. Still, his "mental
alienation" adds potent fire
to his idylls, so Allen, whom Clare
in a snit once dubbed Dr Bottle-Imp,
arranges patronage. July 1841.
Furze, ling and brake all mingling free and grass

forever green. He's looking for it now,
a home in the green world, yet sees hardly
a thing he knows for his own. Overhead
two birds whisk, tight-yellow-wing-tipped warblers,
lighting on a bare yew or plane tree limb.
The Gipseys are gone—one left her hat—so
he stuffs it in his pocket for *another*

opportunitty. Two days later he's
forty miles closer, running parallel

to the Great York Road, passing Labour-
in-Vain public house, then Potton, and a full
view of Bugden. He beds in a gighouse,
trussed down in clover, dreaming of Mary.
Somebody took her away from my side.

It's a buggy day in Ohio, smeared
with humid clouds. I've been hacking back brush,
lopping trees, whizzing my loud weed-eater
down fenceworks and pond's edge to curb the growth.
More and more I recognize the torment
in another's mind better than my own.
I've got a mean streak a mile wide. But why?
I've got a mouthful of weed seeds and bark
and blisters like green grapes in my hands—
gasoline sears the grass-slits up my arms.
But it's nothing a little balm won't soothe,
nothing another pill won't ease. I think
the work does me good, trimming things down
to their marrow-most clarity. When Clare
says he's *feeling very melancholly,*
he means he's been cooped up, half-crazy or
worse for years. He's in love with two women,
Patty and Mary, one real wife and one
beloved in his imaginings—

he misses his children, legitimate
and more. He wants his old life back again
at Helpston on the acres where he wrote,
of beans in blossom, luscious comes their scent.
It makes me less grim to sweat through my shirt
and rip another path among brambles.
It makes me less mean to see Ann happy
now, working inside the picket garden—
she knows the ways of every flowering,

fruit-bearing, food-making thing in the beds
she's raised a foot above the earth. That's where
she wants to be, enclosed and more at ease
by miles than if she were loose in the world
where cracked doors keep her sleepless, where roving
men mean horror and harm. I wish I could
snap my fingers and make it all better.

We're lucky to live at least as latter-
day progeny of medical progress.
Our family's a pharmaceutical
catalog: Adderal, Prozac, Paxil,
Dezyrel, Welbutrin, and the whole pink
genera of antibiotic blooms
that have kept us alive through shock, sepsis,

contagion, the tiniest of toothaches,
the cruelest of terrors. I know our meds
like the life list Clare keeps in his journals.
Got some branches of the spindle tree with
its pink colord berrys that shine beautifully
in the pale sun—found for the first time 'the
herb true love' or 'one berry' in Oxey Wood

brought a root home to set in my garden.
It kills me to think what a decent pill
might have meant to the man. He's ten miles
from home now and hasn't eaten for days.
He's hearing poems in his head, whole poems
at a time, of the thirty-five hundred
he will sing in his lifetime. He thinks he's

Child Harold in this one—sexy, heroic.
In one he grieves he's lost Love home and Mary.
He rips a tuft of grass by the roadside
and writes later it tastes something like bread.
I ate heartily till I was satisfied
and in fact the meal seemed to do me good.
In a life-sketch from Northampton, fellow
patient ("inmate," Clare huffs) G. D. Berry
draws the aged poet sunk in torpor.

He's furrowed, worn, his enlarged cranium
characteristic of long lunacy,
as Allen has it. Even his death mask
will look like a bud about to split open,
eerie smile crackling along the jaw.
In all he'll spend twenty-three years more
in asylum after these runaway days
seeking home—twenty-three years *feeble, lost,*
yet gardening the grounds on hand and knee
and writing poems and letters to ghosts.
Dear Sir I am in a Madhouse I quite
forget your Name or who you are You must
excuse Me for I have nothing To
communicate or tell Of and why I
am shut up I don't know I have Nothing
to say so I conclude Yours respectfully
—he signs it in his finest hand—*John Clare.*
He's almost here. Voices down a gravel walk.
He rests his broken feet on a heap of stone.

What he calls Bedlam Cowslip is lungwort
in our world. I've just splattered the whole batch
beside our fence with my weed-eater, gnats
and dust aspew. If she weren't laughing so
hard, Ann would kill me. But it's nothing

some replanting won't fix. She knows my back's
burning—my head full of whining and rue.

When she calls me to come look, I see
she's unearthed another nest of rabbits.
We could prog them on their way, as Clare writes
in his sonnet on mice, or let them stay
under red flaps of cabbage awhile where
they've feathered the dirt with fur. There's a strong
smell of apples and sweat in the air, scorch

of small engines, the answering yammer
of developers' saws tearing the woods
beyond our green hill. He sees chimney smoke
over the neighbors', a peat-roof. He sees
familiar petals and blades in his yard.
Yet no one's home at his home. He can walk
no more, but wanders the place *nearly hopeless.*

It kills me to think what he knows. He's come
eighty miles in four days, after four lost
years, to find them all gone. O lunatic world.
O lunatic, swelling, flowering world.
He bends to scuff some dirt around her Head-aches—
homeless and home   and half gratified
to feel that I can be happy any where

TWO

Flowers . . . had Tongues.
—*Emily Dickinson*

1.

Hard to picture him here in the lake grass
taking notes, up to his knees in mud, bugs,
but here he is, in Canada, August,
1880, tracing the flights of birds.
Like a bird he takes whatever he finds
to make words, the backs of letters, homemade
notebooks, and writes sometimes without looking
they are so plentiful, the shy *Shore-lark*

and all the Sparrows, Oriole (hanging
bird—golden robin), Scarlet Tanager,
swallows, the (very common) cedar-bird.
Lists, lists enlivening his mind, as his
better father said they would do, for bare
lists of words are found suggestive to an
imaginative and excited mind.
Yet he is half-paralyzed from the strokes

and must hang on to Wm. Sanders's firm arm
to continue. Lists in manuscript are
his poems now, his greatest Leaves fallen
years past, consigned to infamy or fame.
Lists draw their power straight from nature
as from his expressions. *Words of all the Laws*

of the Earth—he closes his eyes to feel
the sun bathe his face, softly now he breathes—

Words of the Sun and Moon,
Words of Geology, ~~Chemistry Gegro~~ *History, Geography,*
Words of ~~Me~~ *the Medieval Races,*
Words of the Progress of ~~Law~~*, Religion, Law, Art, Government,*
Words of the ~~Topography~~ *surface of the Earth, grass, rocks,*
 trees,
  Flowers, grains, and the like,
Words of the Air and Heavens,
Words of the Birds ~~of the~~*, and of insects,*
Words of ~~the~~ *Men and Women—the hundreds of different*
  Nations, tribes, colors, and other distinctions . . .

2.

He's sixty-one, famous, and half-infirm.
He's doted on by Addington Symonds, Bucke,
hounded for his views on Lincoln and life.
Yet now, in Ontario, by the lakes,
he is simply Walt, noting here when one
little black-and-white bird [the goldfinch]
lights from his billowy flight on a low
pine bough not ten feet off. In one gesture

he considers the significant trait
of civilization Benevolence—
and thinks it *doubtful whether ~~it~~ this* is
anywhere illustrated to fuller
degrees than in Ontario, *with its*
countless institutions for the Blind, one
for the Deaf and Dumb, one for Foundlings,
a Reformatory for Girls, one for

women, and no end of homes for the old
and infirm, for waifs, and for the Sick—and
then adjusts the list . . . *(all ~~vario~~ sorts)*
otter, coon, mink, martin, ~~and buffalo~~
musk-rat, &c. Equality
is nature's law and must be government's.
The rich, abundant, wild various hues
of the birds, the hunting hawks, the ruby-

throated whirring hummingbirds, the brave gold-
finch full of song—so many genera—
should not confuse the mind. In his rough-hand
Primer of Words he traces the native
people's phrases found in the north prairies,
their *wardance, powwow, Sachem, Mohekan,*
then notes as in a new poem the fate
of the Africans, the poignant irony . . .

3.

barracoon—
        the collection of slaves
                in Africa, or anywhere
        ("I see the slave barracoon")—
how hybrid songs of "nigger dialect"
have furnished *hundreds of outre ~~names~~
words,* many of them adopted into
the common speech of the mass of people.

In another notebook, in years past, he
fretted with this problem so, writing *I
know there are strong and solid arguments
against slavery—arguments addressed
to the great American thought Will it pay?
We will ~~go directly~~ stand face to face
with the / chief of the supreme bench. We will
speak with the soul.* [new page] *For ~~free~~ as great
        as any worldly wealth to a man,—or*

~~her~~ *womanhood to a woman,—greater
than these, I think, is the right of liberty,
to any and to all men and women.—*
Lists. Lists. Bare words. Nature's compositions
stretch before the receptive eye. He has

found a cool moss-covered slab of limestone
to light on, looking south, over the lake.
Tomorrow, he thinks, he'll speak yet with Bucke

about the poems, perhaps a lecture tour.
There is so much to say about the world.
These grasses, for instance, growing so tall
in the wild—*what are they?* Timothy, joe-
pie weed, ripgut perhaps. Of what nature,
what kind are they? There's another question
here, a hope—he needs to frame this better . . .
how they blow in the wind . . . how they go on . . .

or, *how they may seed.* Yes. How continue.

Here she comes with her face to be kissed. Here she comes
lugging two plastic sacks looped over her arms and stuffed

with fresh shoots. It's barely dawn. She's been out
for an hour already, digging up what she can save

before developers raze the day's lot sites and set woodpiles
ablaze. That's their plan for the ninety-plus acres.

She squats in the sun to show me wild phlox
in pink-running-to-blue, rue anemone, masses

of colt's foot, wild ginger, blood root and may-
apples, bracken and fiddlehead fern—ferns being not

spring ephemerals per se, but imperiled by road graders
come to shave the shaded slopes where they grow.

Once I held her in a snow cover of sheets. Wind beat
the world while we listened. Her back was a sail,

unfurling. She wanted me to touch stitches there,
little scabs, where doctors had sliced the sick cells

and cauterized her skin for safety's sake.
Now her hands are spotted by briars, bubbles of blood

daubed in brown. She's got burrs in her red hair.
Both sleeves are torn. She kneels as the sunlight

cuts through pine needles above us, casting a grid
like the plats the surveyors use. It's the irony

of every cell: that it divides to multiply.
This way the greedy have bought up the land

behind ours to parcel for resale at twenty-
fold what they paid weeks ago.

It's a race to outrun their gas cans and matches,
to line the path to our creek with transplants

of spice bush, yellow fawn lily, to set aside space
in the garden for the frail. She adjusts the map

she's drawn of the tumbling woods—where each
flower and fern come from, under what tree, beside

which ridge. *Dysfunctional junctional nevus*:
a name like a bad joke for the growth on her skin,

pigment too pale for much sunlight. *Drooping trillium*,
she says, handing me a cluster of roots, unfolding leaves—

rare around here. How delicate, a trillium,
whose oils are food for ants, whose sessile leaves are

palm-sized, tripartite. They spread a shadow over
each stem's fragile one bloom, white in most cases,

though this one's maroon. This makes it rarer.
It hangs like a red bell safe from the sun. It bends

like our necks bend, not in grief, not prayer,
as we work with our backs to the trees, as they burn.

Something wrong in the wind. Maybe a storm.
No one said. Something wrong in the faces
of the old people who led us by hand.

Would you be happier playing awhile?—
wild apples so full of blossoms they wept
when we passed, her smokehouse far enough

from the big house we couldn't disturb
the stillnesses there nor see for ourselves.
But the smokehouse scent of hickory high

in the dark corners, but the Ball jars full
of buttons and stays, and her harness tack,
and as though she were passing, a rustle

in the oilskin curtains crisp with half light,
half shadow themselves on the cobbler's bench
—but the two iron heels heels-up in the dark.

More blossoms fell when the wind blew. More piled
on more when we walked through the yard,
a taste of cider at our teeth, but the white

grass, white haze all the way up to the house.
Something wrong when they let us in. Wept dry,
straining not to strain, they cut piece on piece

for us, fruit pies piled onto her table
already stacked high—too much to eat
or carry home or recall. No one said,

but we would learn later, like the blossom
waste of the apples all over the ground,
it was less about plenty than goodness.

WHITE VIOLETS AND COAL MINE

Charles Burchfield (1872–1967)

Even his journals are voluminous, thick
as a masonry brick, yet nowhere
in them does he prefigure the details
of his painting. 1918 finds him
back in Salem, finished at the Cleveland School
of Art, clerking in the cost department
of W. H. Mullins Company,
and growing depressed about his prospects.
He's twenty-five, painting constantly,
everything around him a subject—
burled boughs of trees, abandoned shacks, smokestacks
working in the weather of a storm, all
manner of junk, crickets, clouds, torn trestles,
the outside world rendered in lines and swirls
in all the hues of hallucination.

The men come up at evening for supper.
It's hard to pick them out
by face—smudged black, grubbed
Cyclopes-eyes of their lanterns

snuffed out, one by one, hardly a word
to share in their exhaustion.
The mules have sunk their noses
deep into the troughs. My great-uncle

waits to check their hooves—
his fire and anvil ready, shoes, sledge,
and nails—having straightened a rail
where the track warped.

April 4, 1917. This is
all he wrote—*Thinking of rank fungus growth*
I suddenly saw them in my mind grow
upward in a snaky evil fashion—.
He's terrified by night, by woods, *by roar*
of wind in tree tops, by curling phantom
like slits, studded with stars, the bleak
lonely roadway—Cemetery woods a
rolling bristle of saplings, by what lives,
crawls, flies, or blows in the common winds.
But through all his journals there's only this
about a mine, 1912, 25th
of February . . . *Set in the side of*
the hill here is the Mine, now gone to ruin,
followed here by several lines of description.

I have his nails—square-headed—long
as locust thorns, two irons

he forged, and rivets of a boot sole.
I have his great deep-grained

long-handled toolbox, varnished
like a vanity, open at the top,
which my love's displayed for years
at our picture window as a planter:

ivy, wound in veins across the chest.
I have the horror of my neglect,
the easy life. I dream of someone
I don't know gone down to die.

It's less a mine than a mouth, a torn pit.
The trees, twisted, chopped at their limbs, are black
leaning over the mouth, or are falling,
and wisps of something—smoke, gas, ghosts, claw-marks
cutting their way up from the drear landscape—
waver in threes above the white violets.
This is nowhere good to be, to be
the site for all the coal to fire Ohio's
factories, heat its homes. *Old mines always*
have a luring mysteriousness, but
fear seizes me—as is symptomatic

of the man. The good is warped, worn, or wild.
He has captured this irony as he
observes the dripping water, thawing stone,
the *wild sepulchral beauty of the depths.*

I don't know his whole name.
I never asked. But family wisdom
keeps him with me always,
like the echo of a story—

years of dust, the gas, hammered
bones, and work, always work, back-
killing labor, lungs full of blackness.
And death, quick as a strut

breaking, slow as a mule.
I waken at night sometimes
to see him standing by my bed, gazing
down, arms above his head—.

Whatever fascinates will terrify.
So he paints drooling imps in the elm trees,
and blood pooled, pink, at the feet of surgeons
dazed by what they have done, standing stunned

above a body they've just butchered. Or saved.
Bluebirds along the muddy road—singing
of telegraph—a feeling that spring may
come but nature grows more & more hideous . . .
I know nothing else of a man in
Missouri, who saved his mules' feet to work
each day, who fed his family on dust.
The world is ghosted, waiting to swallow,
so Burchfield paints a mine to show this fact.
It looks almost like somewhere I have been,
including this. His violets are screaming.

The sound was too low-pitched to be singing
or a baby—too far off through the woods.

Stretched on the bottommost step of her porch,
she looked liked she'd been here all day, pulling

weeds from the walk, reading her mysteries.
But when I saw her blouse brightened with tears

and both feet twisted, already swollen,
I knew her good neighbor had called the squad—

one ankle plainly broken, the other
so bad the skin bulged, almost cut, with bone.

Nearly forty years and this the first time
I had cursed in front of her. Jesus Christ!

How long have you been here? Wait, she said.
The hummingbirds . . . back in the coral bells . . .

THREE

Hast thou the heart?
—*Algernon Charles Swinburne*

MELANCHOLY MAN

1.

What makes Robert Burton's *Anatomy of Melancholy*
so hard to put down is his wild branching rhetoric.
It's not enough to trace pathologies of mind, whatever
path a lost mind takes—he wants to make it rhyme,
invest it with the kind of power music makes or minds
in a quandary, and give it memory's crutch mnemonics.
Ingress, progress, regress, egress, much alike, he writes,

citing four culpable causes of "discontents, cares,
miseries, etc.," yet even here his rhyming trochees
don't suffice as art until he finishes the sentence
with a flourish suitable to the Bible or beloved Lucretius:
*blindness seizeth on us in the beginning, labour
in the middle, grief in the end, error in all.*
Root to trunk to limb to leaf—as he might say.

2.

In my friend's voice I hear a ghost.
Home from the hospital, he is, at sixty-two,
scared of his heart's heredity—who wouldn't be?—
a host of uncles dead before their time, his father,
at fifty-six, the four chambers of whose heart

filled with the effluvium of both their lifetimes.
He feels the line stretching to him the way

the branching tree leads or leans, one to the next,
the way the heart goes bad one tapped vein at a time.
Melancholy man, he calls himself, though he has written
of a cloud, even of peaceable clouds in a painting,
it is right to think of these as elegies of the spirit, to see
their forms as melancholy hosts, and the poet watching
clouds is watching phantoms levitating stone.

3.

How hard to hold to a single thought in hand.
Sorrow is one cause but confusion itself is symptom
of the malady—Burton's explanations being one part
medicine, one part art, and clearly confessional
of his brooding mind. *I say fickle, fugitive, they may
not abide to tarry in one place long. Eftsoons pleased,
and anon displeased, as a man that's bitten with fleas.*

Love of learning, he says, is a central cause,
as is, among "accidental sources," too much education.
Thus the sore afflicted go commonly meditating
unto themselves, thus they sit, abroad, aloof, aloft,
senseless to nature and time, and in hopes to recover

must turn rustic, rude, or melancholize alone.
But how hard not to be enchanted with the rhyme.

4.

When his best friend died, at fifty-five, the good heart
deserted its host. It's in his voice, spectral, static
on the line. The heartline of the graph draws
straight to him. Loss of friends is so great a cause,
Burton says, *amongst the Pagan Indians, their wives
and servants voluntarily die with them.*
He sees Bill's ghost, cold, candle-white,

and like a cloud grown abstract—though none of us dies
entirely, he writes, though some of us, all of us sometimes
come back sapling, seedling, cell, like second growth,
he finds himself alone, dead weight of his bones,
standing over graves in moonlight's shadow.
He hears his pulse beat in his ear. Pressed hard,
he says, against the receiver, to see—are you still here?

THE WAVES

A man under water
will breathe water—

one taste, reluctantly,
and then deeply

drinking what he needs
in another form

until it fills him,
the way a smoker,

deep in thought or
desperate, draws breath,

the rush, the chem-
ical enchantment

with its thousand shocks,
its wash of nicotine-

as-adrenaline until
his heart's aflutter

until it's not, as here,
tipping back his head

—three cups beside him:
pills, mashed ice, top teeth—

his heart having sunk
yet the body so

starved for one sip of
oxygen he goes on

trying, taking
his last (the doctor

calls it) agonal
breaths—meaning no air's

pulled in, his jaw
goes down, he nods

in slow ascent, oh
waves, oh fabulous

smoke, oh lovely (our
breath's gone, too)

memory, breathing in.

1. By Heart

    In Galen's anatomical study,
  the heart is not perfectly spherical.
Rather, beginning at its circular
    base above, "called the head," it gradually

    decreases in size "very like a cone."
  This great work requires twenty-two volumes
in modern codex, as *Medicorum*
    Graecorum opera quae exstant

    omnia, to house the wisdom,
  the blood-depth he gathered in the second
century—the gist of whose depictions
    remains standard for hundreds of years, from

    the huge compendium by Arab court
  physician Avicenna, in 1000,
who notes the heart "contracts to a pine-cone"
    (an image upheld in Haly Abbas's heart

    "resembling a pine-cone," in which each of
  the heart's chambers "has two accessory
parts on the outside which look like ears
    and which are called heart ears," which itself moves

the metaphor from tree back to body-
in-miniature, recalling Macrobius's
bladder-shaped heart and Plutarch, who was
struck by the Egyptian plant *persea*

for its "fruit resembles a heart, its leaf
a tongue") to the late fourteenth century,
when heart depictions first portray what we
think of now as the valentine's deep cleft.

One side of the dialogue / I have by heart . . .
                                        —*Chase Twichell*

Our big pine burst
branches, black ice—
shooting, limbs sheathed
needles aglow around
I worked beside my
as more trees snapped
the ice-upon-snow.
against silhouettes of
smudged by blackout.
we stacked gone limbs,
the eaves and shrubs

in the night. White
it blazed out in veins
with ice afire, crystal
the blown transformer.
love in the brute night
in the wrecking wind,
The cold grew darker
our neighbors' windows
Beneath crackling trees,
we shoved ice off
—relieving that burden—

we cut our neighbor's car from beneath his
dropped willow. And when we came in
glistening then, cold, when we made love,
or tried to, my breath blew too quickly still,
my arms, tighter, burned. It was more
than one heart could bear: all of us there.

2. Cardiognosis

No less than Aristotle rendered first
the heart's interior as tri-chambered,
"the largest being on the right hand side,
the smallest on the left" (one thinks, whose left?),

"the medium-sized one in the middle,"
this from his *History of Animals*,
350 B.C. But Galen quarrels
strongly, with a gusto unusual

and blunt: "What wonder that Aristotle,
among his many anatomical
errors, thinks the heart in large animals
has three cavities!" This third ventricle,

he's sure, is just hollow space (*fovea*
in the Latin texts) in the right chamber.

Still, dispute over the interior
   structures grows contentious. Avicenna

      tries to resolve the conflict by putting
   Aristotle's third chamber *into*
Galen's heart, "as it were, *between*" two
   larger chambers, as by a graft, calling

      this part the "non-ventricular meatus,"
   which works as a storehouse for the pneuma
(*spiritus*) generated in it "from
   the subtil blood." Thus, Mondeville's handy

      diagram (1312), etched in his text,
   places the third chamber at the heart's base.
Thereby Johannes Mesue displays his
   heart-rooms not horizontally but stacked

      vertically, then calls them "pouches as
   some purses" have. Through the years, depictions
of the heart's outer shape evolve, fashion
   by fashion, but always maintain these halves,

      until every scheme leads to the deepened
   cleft shape in the fourteenth century. It's

as if, as the heart's interior grows
　　fuller with possibilities, we find

　　　　its exterior grown pronounced by "dips,"
　　"dents," "angular indentations," until
the cloven heart becomes our given style:
　　three chambers inside a double heart-shape

　　　　within a single chest. It's irony
　　befitting a lover, beloved, and "that
which comes between them." The halved heart
　　wants a third. But here's the really funny

　　　　part. Vinken identifies an early
　　Coptic textile (c. 400) showing
a saint, "likely Ezekiel," looking
　　in the air—toward God, one assumes—and sees

　　　　floating there a small rust-colored shape, most
　　surely a heart, with a clear indentation
marking its top like the first valentine.
　　Yet close inspection shows it's not made that

　　　　way—not design, but long wear. It's a tear.

The heart's division divideth us . . .
—Swinburne

When he fell at the rehab gym, they said
he'd overexerted himself, but just

a little rest would "work wonders." Then tests—
poor flow, blockage, something blood thinners fix . . .

then no, they would use their balloons, like toys
threaded up from the groin. We could hardly

breathe, waiting. At last, the MRI
determined, there were *three* problem places

—"too many to play with"—three separate
congested arteries near his great heart,

so they built little ramps for the traffic
to flow more quickly to the center of town.

Ancient solution: bypass the problem.
Thus the Pruefening series, which depicts

"circulation man," an anatomical
study in 1158 struck

in five poses ("none drawn from dissection"),
notable for his heart fixed directly

to his mouth. No lungs, no larynx, few veins,
just as Bodleian-Ashmolean man

(in 1282) shows his "trachea
heart" attached straight to his lips by a tube.

How clarifying our desire: make things
work by making them simple and direct.

Okay, we said. When do we start?

3. The Book of the Heart

    It's hard to overstate the relevance
  of the change—millennia long—from clay
tablet to cloth scroll as the preferred way
    to hold language, scrolls being an advance

in portability, durability,
even artistic possibility.
This seems so little, still, compared to the
evolution of scroll to technically

superior codex: i.e., the book.
Books are the bode of thought, though (Emerson
adds) "not by books alone" are our souls known.
Thus, wandering the desert, as one Coptic

weaver labored at his intricate scene,
generations of holy fathers asked
that their hearts be ready to receive, said
Basil of Caesarea (329–

379), "impressions produced
there by divine instruction." What he means
is, in the dearth of books the desert saints
suffered, lugging their shadows dune to dune,

the heart itself shall be read, runic, clear,
and textual as scripture: the heart as
site of faith and spirit, not merely house
of the blood. The trick, of course, is to clear

the page of sinful text before God's fresh
script "of the new converted soul" can be
overwritten there. One feels the scalding
    sand, the singeing wind, thus the burning flesh

blown off like chaff until only the heart
remains. That, Thomas Watson says in *God's
Anatomy upon Man's Heart*, is God's
    hard judgment. "He has an eye in your heart,

He is *kardiognostes*." Heart-knower.
So the desert fathers executed
the surgery of their souls each day. What
    they saved is archive, exegesis, fear-

into-love as language. And God stands there
(does he stand?) with the twin lobes
of your heart cracked open like a book. *Scribe
    with Heart-Shaped Book*, by the Flemish Master

of Sainte-Gudule (c. 1485),
sanctifies this grand confluence of heart
as text, soul as scribe. The painting's clear art
    says, *Read my heart, forever stay alive.*

My heart's in such disarray / that I am estranged from everyone.
—Azalais de Porcairagues

An hour ago my heart was a curse, burned
fist, wracked metronome, a book—if a book—
of flame. I couldn't catch my breath to breathe.
The inheritance from our elders is
inevitable as weather, as is
the terror of my love for you, my love.
Each day the heart becomes word, an effort,
a blessing as a blessing is a curse,
as writing is belated surgery
for our devotions. I went with my love
into the snow to save our beloved
trees. I lay with my love, in long grasses,
and tasted my body's blood on her tongue.
—Now it's the fifteenth century once more
and Azalais grieves her heart's true song.
She's grown up in the region surrounding
Montpellier, the mid-twelfth century,
is noble, educated, and madly
wrecked by Gui Guerrejat, "the warrior,"
for whom her *cansos* cry. Hers are the most
vivid of all the trobairitz heart-songs,
more personal, more torn than any poems

of her peers. It is all we know of her,
and this: *Now we are come to the cold time*
where there's snow and ice and sludge
and the little birds are mute,
not one attempts to sing,
and the boughs are bare in hedges;
neither flower nor leaf is sprouting there,
nor, calling there, the nightingale
who wakes my soul in May . . .
My heart's in such disarray
that I am estranged from everyone;
I know that we have lost
in less time than it took to gain.
However much we might try, we cannot
absolve the heart its pain. The terror is
not losing you but having you before
you are lost. The terror is, loving you
this way, my body is gone, and the wind
carries my songs, until you are words, too.

Nothing under the black walnut. Nor where
our three hydrangeas share a mild shadow.
Nothing beside the limestone ridge, dry creek,
nor where cuttings from last year's fallen pine
—split in half by ice—freshened enough spores
to germinate a rich crop of morels.
They're usually a perennial growth.
We depend on them thus for our pleasure,

cooked to our liking, sautéed with a spoon
of garlic over noodles, slow-fried in
egg batter like an omelet, but also
for the sheer delight of their springing up
in the soft humus, the leaf-spoil of woods,
or near some new mayapples unfisting
so green they glow. So if we count on them,
does their absence account for a loss?

Legally yes. That's the way the lawyers
will add up the worth and shortfalls of our
marriage, should it go, too. Not only what
we have, but what we would have had. Income,
children, happiness, and death. Even sex
—sex we would have had—measurable
as money on a standard pro-rated
by expectation and level-of-life . . .

sex, whose absence is calculable, in-
curable, and called our "hedonic loss."
It's just that way this year, our friends will say.
The weather. Or the cycles. Or the fates.
Nothing by the apple trees. Nor where old
barns have crumbled into mulch and flowers.
Nothing is left but what is lost. And I
will go on missing you until I die.

It is finished now, it is begun, this
on which he one
    Isaac Newton, Esq.,
    sonne of Isaac and Hanna baptiz'd
    Jan 1 anno 1642
imprest this page his first with wetted lips.
Thus he anoints his book, *The Waste Book,*
    better able to keep
    records recollections Calculations

as such that nothing's lost nor goes surpassed,
since *Absolute,*
    true, and mathematical
    Time, without reference to anything
    external, flows uniformly. From his hand
pour onto the page axioms, numbers,
sometimes figurations to the length
    of fifty-five decimals,
    on another two thousand crabbed digits

marching in ordered formation—if smudged
by a palm—elsewhere
    hasty confusion
    in creation's best wording: *as the body*
    (a) is to the body (b) so must the

power of efficacy vigor strength
or virtue of the case which begets the same
      quantity of velo-
        city . . . &c. He's twenty-one,

home from Cambridge (shut to the Pestilence),
writing with the
      force of new Excitements
      in his thousand-page book. The real Fluxion
      of things makes their Inclination toward
each other an Attraction, as bodies in
Motion so attract, thus Mars Venus Jupiter
      &c. to the Sun.
      He ponders, slows his quill, observing now

a farmwife dropping slosh from a bucket . . .
repellant woman—.
      What a great gift
      Apothecary Clarke has made, who left
      this paper, taught him to grind by pestle
and mortar the world's matter, to burn
chemicals into pellets. There is
      Genesis in the hand,
      as in the Circulating mind. *This is very*

agreeable to natures proceedings,
for as planets
      orbit, so do Seeds
      in alchemy. It's the secret to his
      science that from bodies in Conjunction
new values rise. *Nothing is produced from*
masculine or feminine semen alone.
      Even opposites—
      Pression & Fluxion, Attraction &

Repulsion, Heat & Cold—may by violent
burning be imprest
      into a ferment,
      then be transformed, as may Mercury (as
      quicksilver) into Gold. And yet he burns,
as any body burns, with that other
natural proximity. *The way to*
      chastity is not to
      struggle directly with incontinent

thoughts but to avert the thoughts by some
imployment, or
      by reading, or meditating . . .
      He turns distempered, *embroild.* He spends years
      fuming in his seclusion, *seeing*

apparitions of woemen and their shapes . . .
Even his great *Principia*, made of
    Latin's logic and pure
    numbers, becomes a form of celibacy.

There goes, one Cambridge student is heard
to mutter, *the man*
    that writ a book
    that neither he nor anybody else
    understands. Yet when the coinage of
the empire fails, he emerges quickened
into power, an older public man.
    As Warden of the Mint,
    1696, he recasts the nation's wealth,

charcoal fires burning around the clock . . .
Soon the Trial of Pyx—
    soon his beknighted
    rise to Curator of Experiments
    for the Royal Society: as all these
years before he finds the truth in alchemy.
I know whereof I write for I have in
    the fire manifold
    glasses with gold and this new Mercury.

By its continued Circulation, gold
begins to swell,
    to be swollen. From his
    fingers issue Visions Stars . . . Thus his estate,
      when he dies, at eighty-four—two thousand
books, one clock, mathematical appliances,
hordes of coins, wine, hidden Gold Barrs, his whole
    household upholstered
      in crimson—staggers the empire: precisely

31,821
pounds. *All must be*
    used. He taps his pen. Good,
    he thinks, *I reckon this a great secret.*
    Now the hag has emptied her slosh-pail and gone—
and he sets forth alone on his great book
with a deeper concentration, the
    Philosophic mercury,
      the seminal Fires, burning anew . . .

FOUR

The matter of the heavens is fluid.

—*Isaac Newton*

If this were the sea and not snow, morning-
cold, Ohio, the slick black trees standing
for themselves along our ice creek, then
these birds might seem ready for the flight.
They've opened their massive wings, five,
six feet across, and hold them to the cold sun
as though cutting through salt winds unfettered.
This dries them. But how eerie they look,
like the stonework of graves, like gargoyles
dripping and grim in the precision of faith.
They have settled on just one tree. Sunlit,
they are black blooms, their heads wrinkled
as walnuts, each with a small smear of blood
for a face. If this were the sea. But it's not.
If she were alive and yesterday's procession
of black cars, flutter of flags, were something
other than what they were, like wisps of smoke
sent up from the steamer churning for home,
then we might know at least the gods await.
That the ash does cleanse. And the afterlife
shall yield us great wings for the body
to fly where the others, it seems, have gone.

THE EVIDENCE

In the first weeks,
they wanted
for nothing.
This is how

it always is—
bountiful body,
ravenous laws.
They watched

at the curb
as the horse
parade passed:
colorful flags, fanfare,

such clapping.
They called to
the elderly couple
across the way,

raising their
pale hands
each morning
and evening, as to

an old question.
They took on
each other's
likeness with joy.

Thus the good days
sweep lightly,
like scented limbs
of pear trees beside

the front windows.
This is how it
always is.
And so clearly

the evidence
gathers, green
being what
green leaves repel.

We wade into a blackened pond to save
      the dying water.
      The water isn't dying
—we know, we know—it's the fish and frogs
      starving, pushed out
      by subsurface growth.

Still, that's how they put it to us,
      our new neighbors
      who've come
to watch us cope with our
      stagnant, weedy, quarter-acre
      runoff swamp.

They say let it go, by which they mean
      (this from Scott, cut
      like a side of beef,
six-pack belted like a holster to his pants)
      it's God's will, or nature's, and besides
      it's too much work,

to which his father John, bigger, bald
      scorch of a face, plops
      on our dock and says you

got that right. At first we tried sprinkling
      chemicals around
      the darkening perimeter—to wit,

copper sulfate penta-
      hydrate ($CuSO_4$-$5H_2O$),
      used variously as
a micronized fungicide in pellets,
      a crystalline pesticide "noted
      for acute toxicity in bees,"

and here, a powdery "powerhouse" algaecide—
      or in other words (this
      from John), fancy sunblock
for the water. For weeks the bottom-
      black surface glowed
      eerily aquamarine,

yet all that died were two fat grass carp,
      lazy from the slime
      they ate, who floated up
like scaly logs to petrify. That's why
      I'm waist-deep
      where my neighbors watch,

rowing with a rake through
      a sludge of leaves,
        stirring algae
in a cooking pot. Each time I pull a gob
      of slime and glop, dark
        as organs, toward shore,

John yells out, encouraging, *that's* a good one,
      and I shove it on to Ann
        to rake up the bank
where we can haul it off sometime.
      Don't just sit there
        in the willow shade,

I ought to shout. Come on. Help us out.
      Or (this from Virgil via
        Corydon), why not at least
go about some needful task? But there's
      so much trouble
        in the world these days

I've been content to work in peace
      beside my wife, my life's
        surprising love,

to keep the cardinals throbbing in our close cattails
      and frogs at home
      in a splash of breathable water.

Each step stirs a slick
      of spreading ooze
      that follows
orbital in my wake, nebulae of oil
      and algae stars. And look,
      overhead the first real star

has answered back: There's darkness
      on the way. We drag another
      sloppy mass up the bank
and see its dimming possibilities—
      tadpoles and minnows,
      shiny as coins, egg-

clusters of sun perch, bluegill roe—
      throbbing in the grass,
      twisting to be loose, aglow
against the color of the coming night. And there go
      John and Scott, down
      on their knees in the grass,

untangling as many as they can to slip back
     to the black pond, before the sky
     turns black as well.
There's smoke you can see from the neighbors' chimney,
     and the shadows of the hills are
     lengthening as they fall.

Color of dusk's summer sky, the rain clouds fading yet coming on,
color of nothing or nothing's neutral gray sibling shadow,

so the small bird seemed, sitting on a wire, part of this weather,
neither wren nor vesper sparrow, though no larger than these,

this moment, in a drought, in the dusk, when the gnats were a cloud
hoping to feed on the hard tomatoes, the pink-black-lined

rose mallows and bitter rhododendrons, before the night air grew
fretful with bats. This is where we were when they called to say,

first, she was still alive, then barely so. A bird in these moments
flew down. Or not so much flew as dropped, engaged its wings,

swooped to pick a thing out of the air, then flipped back to a wire
or off sometimes to a hole in the sheltering, high pine.

Hunger drives the animal mind to fill its needs by the nearest means.
Dusk, sky, the look of rain above our own backyard—we stayed

a moment longer—and the woods-edge melting
in the world's shadow. And the brown deer stepping out of
    the woods.

OCTOBER STORM

1.

The green sky,
  the gray-green sky
  growling now,

the first stone-
  gray rain pellets
  starting down,

so he looped
  his leg over
  a fence-rail

to watch from
  the weed safety
  of the side

and I walked
  out—Carl wouldn't
  go—to fetch

the colt wild
  from a week at
  pasture alone.

What more? You'd
      gone to your chore.
      Knuckle of

stone to de-
      ice the trough, leaves
      in low whirls,

grist of dust.
      Thunder coming.
      His friend—

they liked the
      word in knowing
      company,

no longer
      code for a covert
      thing, but kitsch,

like a long
      scar, healed enough
      to amuse—

his friend was
      at the barn door
      watching you

work the black
      water in the trough,
      and turned.

Thunder com-
      ing. And then
      the colt was

2.

beside me,
      pulling up snow-
      eyed, slickened

with frenzy.
      What more than to
      raise my arm?

It tells him
      I'm bigger. Easy.
      All right.

But then I
        turned my back,
        the rain driving

mane after
        mane flung full a-
        cross the field,

the sky no
        color I could
        see—down-shove

of wind and
        lightning all at
        once. I saw

the shock of
        a man's face as
        teeth tore through

wet flannel
        to my side,
        the young horse,

teeth bared, fright-
       ened by the
       fury, as

in battle—.
          I pulled him on,
       to the barn,

where you were,
       love. All of us,
       stunned

at the nature
       of the strike . . .
       Storm, then calm.

Nothing else
       but to heal. No-
       thing to keep

from the watchers
       at the gate,
       ever more.

F I V E

Show me your environment
and I will tell you who you are.
— Boris Pasternak

heron is gray, not blue, but great enough
against brown-tipped bowed cattails to be
well-named, is known for its stealth, shier
than a cloud, but won't fly or float away
when it's scared, stands there thinking maybe
it's invisible though it's not—tall, gray,
straight as a pole among the cloudy reeds.

Then it picks up one stem leg. This takes time.
And sets it down just beyond the other,
no splash, breath of a ripple, goes on
slowly across the silt, mud, algae-
throttled surface, through sedge grass,
to stand to its knees in water turning
grayer now that afternoon is evening.

Now that afternoon is evening
the gray heron turns blue, bluer than sky,
bluer than the mercury blue-black still pond.
So when did it snag the bullfrog
hanging, kicking, in its scissor beak?
To look so long means to miss the sudden.
It strides around like a sleek cat

from pond to bank and back, blue tall bird,
washing the frog, banging it against stones,

pecking almost as if it doesn't know
what to do now that it's caught such a thing.
How fast its beak must be to shoot out
like an arrow or that certain—as it's called—
slant of light. Blue light. Where did it go?

Our botanist neighbor's new divorce has
damaged her, she says, in ways she hardly
comprehends. She's helping me cut a path
through the acre of wasteland to my creek.

She calls it *mutualism*, whereby
each thing takes part in the well-being of
each other thing within its local sphere.
The other name for this phenomenon

—she hacks a branch—is *sympathetic
biozone*, meaning, as we know, our back-
woods briars are a self-supporting wild
system. Meaning pawpaws grow tall here

among bramble roses, dense grapevines, thorned
haw and needle locust, and bear their fruit
richly out of reach above the tangle.
I can tell she doesn't want to show how

much she hurts. She's been my friend for years
and whacks—that asshole—a chunk of bramble.
It's taken us two days, so far, three shirts
shredded, leather gloves and jeans despite

the stupid heat, to find the way to cut
through the crap isn't to slice straight into
the stalks and vines. Hit the ropy stems,
the muscle mass of haw and grape, straight across,

and machetes bounce as off a rubber wall.
You've got to make the cut acute. Off
the thorny sections fall, sliced along the slant—
even still, locust and ivy will wrap

around themselves until you ream them out
by hand and drag the mess to your burn pile.
At least the pawpaw lops off like a piece
of willing meat. That's the horror. Something

always eats a system from within.
All I want is a path down to the creek
where my daughter can hide more easily
among the stones, hunt crawdads, sing the songs

she likes to make up when she's alone, or
thinks she is. There's one about a groundhog,
I tell my friend, who's slumped against a trunk,
bleeding from a cheek. It lives in these woods.

It takes its babies up a tree at night
to watch the stars, and sometimes they sprout
red wings. They fly away. They don't return.
That part breaks my heart, I tell my friend. She

tells me back—whack—I know just what you mean.

They push through the dome of the silo.
Or where the dome would be had it not
fallen through, seasons ago, had the sun
not sweetened acorns cast on the floor.
Here she stood, gun in hand like a rake.
Here he prayed, rain or dirt, depending.
Sometimes there is nothing left to say.

The oaks leaf out in a green parasol.
Over what? A beach of bruised refuse,
field waste of honeysuckle and creeper-
vines like manor ivy crawling the walls.
The pump house caved-in, square-headed
nails, brown bottles strewn as by storm,
timber, hewn stone in a rune overgrown—

there is always something more to say,
somebody trying to say it. The barn is
just a rooftop, a cornice in the ground.
How fitting for those driven down,
even a barn, even a house, to their knees.
Here were their lives over which stands
nothing now but a silo sprouting trees.

1.

At first only fog lifting off
the snow and snow
  sifting through it,
  then Pepper pointing to the last

pocket of night among
the densest pines,
  each life for an instant
  in calm regard of the other, and the deep breath

shuddered—the *whomff*—the stern
explosion meant
  not to startle but warn,
  so the big doe stood her ground, then

ran. Or not, being lame, she being
the solitary deer
  four times this week
  up close to the house with her three-

footed hobble, her track
with its triplet prints
  and unmistakable scuff
  where a back leg drags through the drifts.

There's nothing below
where the slender knee should be.
      Nonetheless,
      she has vanished, shadow among shadows

back to the woods, taking her tattered
rags of breath,
      a fluff of tail,
      the sheltie straining at his leash.

2.

And of that sound,
what can I tell you?—
      lingering deep
      as a bear's, drawn up from the gut, chest

broadened until her breath blows out
with great force, plosive
      at the nose.
      The sound's like the *swumpp* of snow sliding

off the eaves, inevitable action-at-
a-distance
      of gravity
      from spring's slow melt.

The ancients thought such behaviors were
rooted in the nature of things
        in themselves
            —arrows dying, a stone in the creek—whose counter-

weight they saw in a floating feather
as levity,
        as in wood, wind, or
            the spirit of the doomed and beloved arising.

My hunter neighbor says
the sound is a feature
        of wilder
            deer. Not those accustomed to our houses and smells,

our noise, who sift softly among
trash cans and orchards
        and flee
            before we know they're among us.

3.

It's the acorns she comes for,
there being nothing to eat
        in the woods,
            the woods being iced over, snow-solid, for weeks.

I have found
only
      the gnawed and spat
      splatter of hedge apples, that's how desperate

they are, driven toward us
by nothing to forage,
      by vanishing trees
      and razed fields, by exurbs, by white-

flight and our insatiate hunger for size
and space and tax
      advantages. She grubs down,
      she snuffles under oaks, blowing back snow

to chew the hard nubbin acorns
though they're frozen,
      squirrel-hollowed,
      and sparse. I have watched her

from my dark window.
I have felt the gravity of her days.
      Little
      remains. We have

a new dog, did I tell you?
He bears
        his lineage well—from those pastoral herders
        of ancient highlands, who

accompanied us, who helped us,
and who from a distance seem almost
        —wouldn't you say it's still so?—
        to float.

Either the cicadas hushed,
or I fell asleep
as they kept on.
      But I go on
      hearing them

in willows, in wild ancient oaks,
in the slow orbit
of my sleep or waking,
      where I lie beside
      White Heron Pond.

Wind whirls through the marsh grasses.
And the slender,
glass wings
      of ten thousand
      insects flare

in the shadows and circulating air,
the throb and ebb
of their song.
      Who says poetry must
      stick to the theme?

asks Su Shih when he looks again
at the painting
he loves—
>   branches of
>   flowering plum.

Burrowing out of
soft ground,
up to the highest limbs,
>   the cicadas
>   mate and sing,

then bear their young, who fall
to earth
to nest, asleep,
>   for seventeen
>   years.

Over algae and moss
of the pond's
still surface,
>   over fields of beans
>   and sweet fescue,

this song wavers and floats—
so Su Shih, after years
migrating
        the provinces, a minor
        official, turns

into Su Tung-p'o, the poet—
or as now, like
the swirl of stars,
        as in my dream
        or waking,

over sun-tipped blooms, over new pipes
poking through
rye grasses,
        over paved
        curbs

running wild into the woods,
the sure, slow
orbit of things
        becoming
        the next thing.

NOTES

"The Judas-Horse": In 1832 George Catlin left Philadelphia, abandoning at the age of thirty-three a promising career as a portrait and miniature painter, and headed West to study "Indian country." From 1832 to 1839 he traveled throughout the Great Plains, sketching and painting hundreds of studies of people, animals, and landscapes. In 1842 he published the first edition of his extensive narrative, *Letters and Notes on the Manners, Customs, and Conditions of North American Indians.* Several phrases and details in this poem come from Catlin's text.

"Bedlam": I use a variety of material from John Clare, including his poems ("The Beans in Blossom," "Emmonsales Heath," "I found a ball of grass among the hay," "An Invite to Eternity," Song A from "Two Songs from Child Harold," and "Two Songs and Some Stanzas from Child Harold"), as well as several passages from his letters, journals, and his "Journey out of Essex." This last text presents Clare's account of his "escape" from the Northampton asylum, his long walk home, and his discovery of his vacant house and lost family. I am indebted to Jonathan Bate's recent work on Clare, especially *John Clare: A Biography* (2003), and to Eric Robinson and David Power for their edited volume of Clare's autobiographical prose works, *John Clare: By Himself* (1996). "Head-aches" is Clare's term for poppies.

"Primer of Words": The primary incident of this poem is a reenactment of an instance during Walt Whitman's journey, in the summer of 1880, as he explored the lakes and landscape of southeastern Canada. I have used phrases from several of his manuscripts and daybooks, including *Daybooks, 1876–November, 1881*; *Diary in Canada*; *The Primer of Words*; and *Other Notebooks, &c. on Words*. The crossed-out passages are as Whitman wrote and revised them. The phrase from Emerson comes from "The Poet."

"White Violets and Coal Mine" takes its title from a painting by Charles Burchfield (1872–1967), who grew up in Ohio and from whose journals and letters some of these passages and accounts are drawn.

"Melancholy Man" is dedicated to Stanley Plumly and adapts phrases from several of his poems. My primary source is Robert Burton's *Anatomy of Melancholy*, the seminal study of early cognitive science and psychology. First published in 1621, it was reissued several times in growing editions, eventually running to nearly half a million words. Roy Porter's *Madness: A Brief History* (2002) and Jennifer Radden's *The Nature of Melancholy: From Aristotle to Kristeva* (2000) were helpful.

"Cardiognosis": Among the many sources I read and used, two were of special help. Pierre Vinken's *The Shape of the Heart* (2000, translated by Peter Mason) is a study of the long history of anatomical depictions of the human heart, its functions and meanings. Eric Jager's *The Book of the Heart* (2000) traces the relationships—during the late medieval era and the Middle Ages—of religious faith, erotic love, reading, and the construction of textual material. I use a phrase in this poem from Anne Carson's *Eros the Bittersweet* and another from Emerson's "Self-Reliance." Azalais de Porcairagues's lines come from her poem "Ar em al freg temps vengut," from *Songs of the Women Troubadours* (2000), translated by Matilda Bruckner,

Laurie Shepard, and Sarah White. I am grateful to Ben Doyle for his timely gift of R. L. Alsaker's *Curing Diseases of Heart and Arteries* (1924), a strange and affecting study of coronary treatment.

"Alchemical Man": I am grateful for information supplied by several biographies of Isaac Newton, especially James Gleick's *Isaac Newton* (2003). I employ quotations, ideas, and procedures from many of Newton's works, including "Clavis," "Quaestiones Quaedam Philosophicae," *Praxis*, "De Aere et Aethere," *The System of the World*, *Mathematical Principles of Natural Philosophy* (*Philosophiae Naturalis Principia Mathematica*)—widely known as *The Principia*—as well as his early handmade *Waste Book*. The practice of alchemy during Newton's lifetime was considered closer to the highest aspirations of both chemistry and religion than to witchcraft or mere whimsy.

"Midwest Eclogue": The question from Corydon is from Virgil's Eclogue II, as Corydon, chiding himself, sings of his hopeless love of Alexis. The last sentence of my poem is from Virgil's Eclogue I, as Tityrus concludes his initial dialogue with Meliboeus. These passages come from David Ferry's translation, *The Eclogues of Virgil* (1999).

"October Storm" is dedicated to Carl Phillips, Doug Macomber, and Mercury.

"Late Pastoral" is dedicated to Linda Gregerson.

"White Heron Pond": The title derives from Su Tung-Po's "White Crane Hills," written in 1097. I also use a line from Su's 1087 poem, "Who Says a Poem Must Look Like Life?" Both were translated by Burton Watson. My poem is dedicated to William Heyen.

David Baker is the author of seven previous books of poems, *Treatise on Touch: Selected Poems* (2005), *Changeable Thunder* (2001), *The Truth about Small Towns* (1998), *After the Reunion* (1994), *Sweet Home, Saturday Night* (1991), *Haunts* (1985), and *Laws of the Land* (1981). His two critical books are *Heresy and the Ideal: On Contemporary Poetry* (2000) and *Meter in English: A Critical Engagement* (1996). Among his awards are fellowships and prizes from the John Simon Guggenheim Memorial Foundation, National Endowment for the Arts, Ohio Arts Council, Society of Midland Authors, Poetry Society of America, and the Pushcart Foundation. His poems and essays appear in such magazines as *The Atlantic Monthly*, *DoubleTake*, *The Nation*, *The New Republic*, *The New Yorker*, *The Paris Review*, *Poetry*, and many others. Baker was raised in Missouri and currently resides in Granville, Ohio, where he serves as poetry editor of *The Kenyon Review*. He teaches at Denison University and in the MFA program for writers at Warren Wilson College.